Compass Point

Phonics Readers

Magnets

by Wiley Blevins

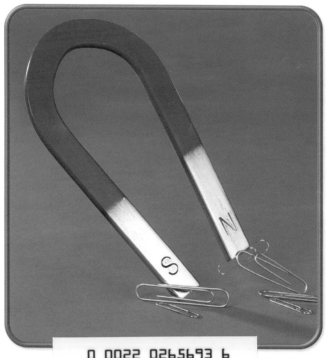

Reading Consultant: Wiley Blevins, M.A.
Phonics/Early Reading Specialist

Compass Point Books
3109 West 50th Street, #115
Minneapolis, MN 55410

Visit Compass Point Books on the Internet at *www.compasspointbooks.com*
or e-mail your request to *custserv@compasspointbooks.com*

Photographs ©: Cover–p. 8, p. 10, p. 11, p. 12: Capstone Press/Gary Sundermeyer, p. 9: David
R. Frazier Photolibrary

Editorial Development: Alice Dickstein, Alice Boynton
Photo Researcher: Wanda Winch
Design/Page Production: Silver Editions, Inc.

Library of Congress Cataloging-in-Publication Data
Blevins, Wiley.
  Magnets / by Wiley Blevins.
    p. cm. — (Compass Point phonics readers)
  Includes index.
  Summary: A simple introduction to magnets, using an easy-to-read text
that incorporates phonics instruction.
  ISBN 0-7565-0511-9 (hardcover : alk. paper)
  1. Magnets—Juvenile literature. 2. Reading—Phonetic
method—Juvenile literature. [1. Magnets. 2. Reading—Phonetic method.]
  I. Title. II. Series.
  QC757.5.B54 2004
  538'.4—dc21   2003006355

Table of Contents

Dear Parent or Caregiver,

Welcome to Compass Point Phonics Readers, books of information for young children. Each book concentrates on specific phonic sounds and words commonly found in beginning reading materials. Featuring eye-catching photographs, every book explores a single science or social studies concept that is sure to grab a child's interest.

So snuggle up with your child, and let's begin. Start by reading aloud the Mother Goose nursery rhyme on the next page. As you read, stress the words in dark type. These are the words that contain the phonic sounds featured in this book. After several readings, pause before the rhyming words, and let your child chime in.

Now let's read *Magnets*. If your child is a beginning reader, have him or her first read it silently. Then ask your child to read it aloud. For children who are not yet reading, read the book aloud as you run your finger under the words. Ask your child to imitate, or "echo," what he or she has just heard.

Discussing the book's content with your child:
Explain to your child that magnets can pull, or attract, iron objects through materials such as paper, cloth, glass, and water. They do not attract objects made of other materials. People use magnets to hold things closed and to lift things.

At the back of the book is a fun Concentration game. Your child will take pride in demonstrating his or her mastery of the phonic sounds and the high-frequency words.

Enjoy Compass Point Phonics Readers and watch your child read and learn!

Going to St. Ives

As I was going to St. **Ives,**
I met a man with seven **wives,**
Every **wife** had seven sacks,
Every sack had seven cats,
Every cat had seven kits,
Kits, cats, sack, and **wives,**
How many were going to St. **Ives?**

A magnet can pick up a pin.
It can pick up a clip, too.

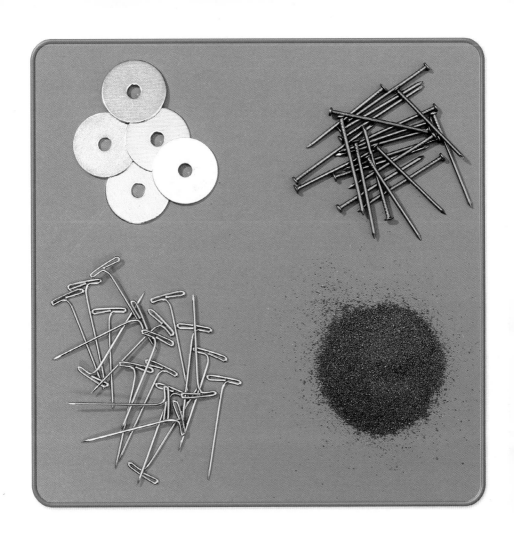

The pin and clip are iron.
Iron is a metal.

Use a magnet on the note.
The note will not slip or slide.

A magnet can be any size.
It can be big.

A magnet can't pick up a rope.
It can't pick up glass.

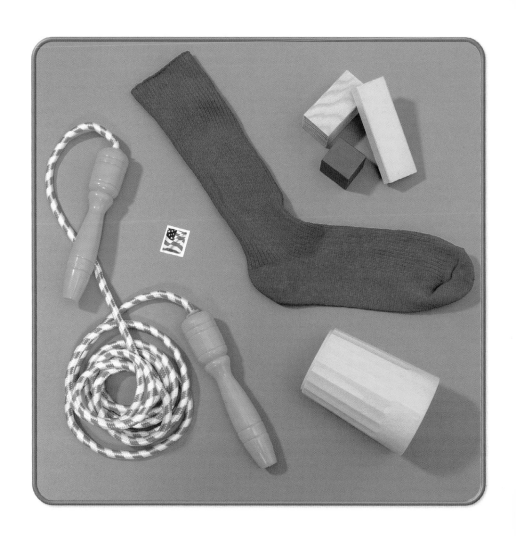

They are not made of metal.

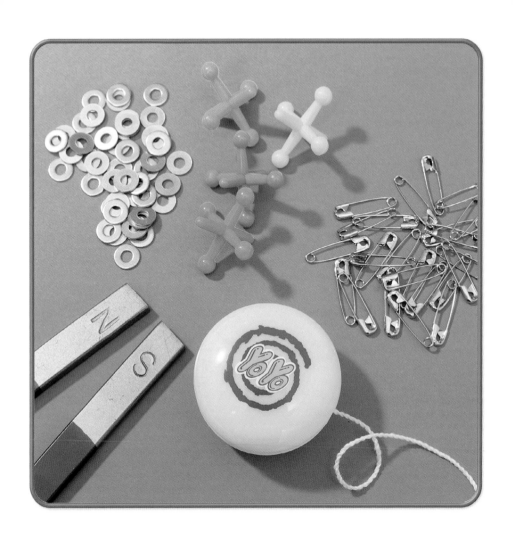

What can a magnet pick up?

Word List

Final *e*

made
note
rope
size
slide
use

l-Blends

clip
glass
slide
slip

High-Frequency

any
are
be
or

Science

iron
metal

Concentration

You will need:
- 16 game pieces, such as pennies or checkers

 note

 glass

 use

 size

 made

 rope

 note

 slip

How to Play

- Cover the words with the game pieces. Players take turns uncovering one word and reading it, then uncovering another word and reading it. If the 2 words are the same, the player takes the game pieces. If the 2 words are not the same, the player covers them with the game pieces, and the next player goes.
- Play until all word pairs have been uncovered. The player with the most game pieces wins.

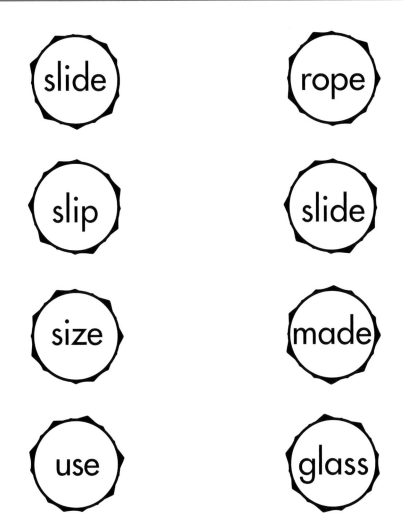

Read More

Oxlade, Chris. *Metal.* Chicago, Ill.: Heinemann Library, 2001.

Rosinsky, Natalie M. *Magnets: Pulling Together, Pushing Apart.* Minneapolis, Minn.: Picture Window Books, 2003.

Royston, Angela. *Magnetic and Nonmagnetic.* Chicago, Ill.: Heinemann Library, 2003.

Stille, Darlene R. *Magnets.* Simply Science Series. Minneapolis, Minn.: Compass Point Books, 2001.

Index